UKULELE

Christmas with Disney

T0081316

ISBN 978-1-4803-9362-2

WALT DISNEY MUSIC COMPANY
WONDERLAND MUSIC COMPANY, INC.

DISTRIBUTED BY

HAL•LEONARD®
CORPORATION

7777 W. BLUEMOUND RD. P.O. BOX 13819 MILWAUKEE, WI 53213

Visit Hal Leonard Online at
www.halleonard.com

Christmas with Disney

Here Comes Santa Claus
(Right Down Santa Claus Lane)

Words and Music by Gene Autry and Oakley Haldeman

First note

Verse
Moderately bright, in 2

1. Here comes San - ta Claus! Here comes San - ta Claus! Right down San - ta Claus
3. Here comes San - ta Claus! Here comes San - ta Claus! Right down San - ta Claus

Lane!   Vix - en and Blitz - en and all   his   rein - deer are
Lane!   He   does - n't care   if you're rich   or   poor   for   he

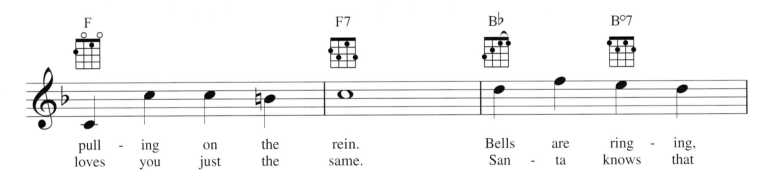

pull - ing   on   the   rein.   Bells   are   ring -   ing,
loves   you   just   the   same.   San -   ta   knows   that

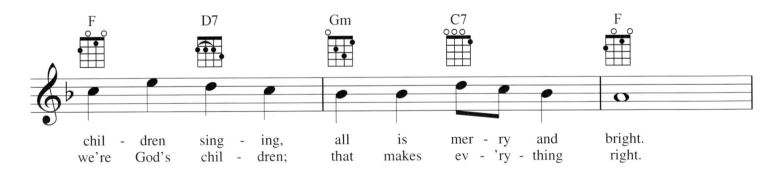

chil - dren   sing - ing,   all   is   mer - ry   and   bright.
we're God's chil - dren;   that makes   ev - 'ry - thing   right.

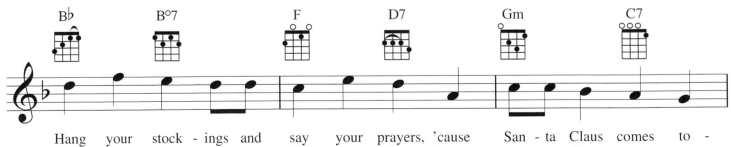

Hang   your   stock - ings and   say   your   prayers, 'cause San - ta Claus comes to -
Fill   your   hearts with   a   Christ - mas cheer, 'cause San - ta Claus comes to -

night. 2. Here comes San - ta Claus! Here comes San - ta Claus!

night. 4. Here comes San - ta Claus! Here comes San - ta Claus!

Right down San - ta Claus Lane! He's got a bag that is

Right down San - ta Claus Lane! He'll come a - round when the

filled with toys for the boys and girls a - gain.

chimes ring out, then it's Christ - mas morn a - gain.

Hear those sleigh - bells jin - gle jan - gle; what a beau - ti - ful

Peace on earth will come to all if we just fol - low the

sight! Jump in bed, cov - er up your head, 'cause

light. Let's give thanks to the Lord a - bove, 'cause

1.

San - ta Claus comes to - night.

2.

San - ta Claus comes to - night.

The Twelve Days of Christmas

Traditional English Carol

1. On the first day of Christ - mas, my true love gave to me: a par - tridge __ in a pear tree.

2. On the sec - ond day of Christ - mas, my true love gave to me:
3. On the third __ day of Christ - mas, my true love gave to me:
4. On the fourth __ day of Christ - mas, my true love gave to me:

Repeat as needed

two tur - tle - doves,
three French __ hens,
four call - ing birds,

and a par - tridge __ in a pear tree.

5. On the fifth day of Christ - mas, my true love gave to me:

Verse

6. On the sixth day of Christ-mas, my true love gave to me:
7. On the sev-enth day of Christ-mas, my true love gave to me:
8.–12. *See additional lyrics*

Repeat as needed

six geese a-lay-ing,
sev-en swans a-swim-ming, } five gold-en rings,

four _____ call-ing birds, three French hens,

two _____ tur-tle-doves, and a par-tridge _ in a pear tree.

Additional Lyrics

8. On the eighth day... eight maids a-milking...
9. On the ninth day... nine ladies dancing...
10. On the tenth day... ten lords a-leaping...
11. On the 'leventh day... 'leven pipers piping...
12. On the twelfth day... twelve drummers drumming...

Jingle Bells / Sleigh Ride Through the Snow

Traditional
Arranged by Richard Friedman

jin - gle bells, jin - gle all the way.

Oh, what fun it is to ride in a one - horse o - pen

sleigh. _____ Jin - gle bells, jin - gle bells,

jin - gle all the way. Oh, what fun it

is to ride in a one - horse o - pen

SLEIGH RIDE THROUGH THE SNOW

Words and Music by Andy DiTaranto and Samuel J. Wisner

Bouncy Doo-Wop, same tempo

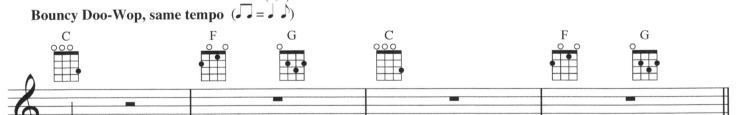

sleigh. *(Spoken:) Gosh, the snow looks beautiful! Aye, that it does.*

Verse

1. We're rid - ing through the snow in a one - horse sleigh ride.
2. So come a - long with us, you'll be de - light - ed in a one - horse sleigh. Gid - dy - up, let's go on a

With a clip - pi - ty - clop, how we love to go on a

hol - i - day sleigh ride through the snow. Jin - gle bells
hol - i - day sleigh ride through the snow. Tell all your

ring - ing and good friends a - long - side. Eat - ing
friends that ev - 'ry - one's in - vit - ed for

gin - ger - bread cook - ies, say - ing hel - lo on a hol - i - day sleigh ride
gin - ger - bread cook - ies, hot co - coa, on a hol - i - day sleigh ride

Pre-Chorus

through the snow.   We'll turn down San - ta Claus Lane and
through the snow.   And now we'll make this ride a

sing some Christ - mas car - ols.   We'll laugh the
hol - i - day tra - di - tion.   Each year, we'll

whole day through,   'cause it's the sea - son to have
wait for you,

Chorus

fun.   Let's go   on a sleigh ride through the

snow.   For - get your shop - pin', we're jin - gle

hop - pin' a - round the town and hav - ing fun.   Let's

Rudolph the Red-Nosed Reindeer

Music and Lyrics by Johnny Marks

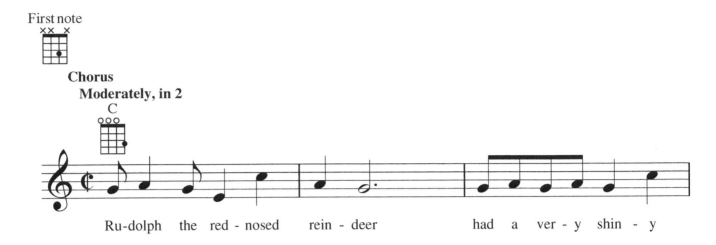

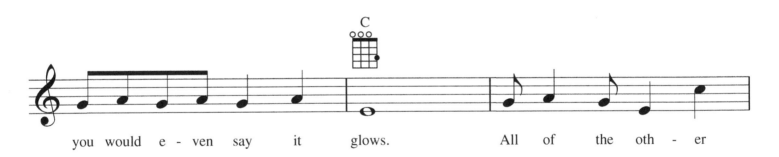

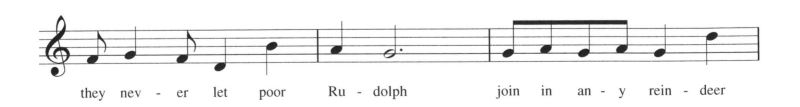

Frosty the Snow Man

Words and Music by Steve Nelson and Jack Rollins

Outro-Verse

mag - ic in that old silk hat they found, for when they placed it
streets of town right to the traf - fic cop, and he on - ly paused a

on his head he be - gan to dance a - round. Oh, Frost - y the
mo - ment when __ he heard him hol - ler, "Stop!" For Frost - y the

Snow Man was a - live as he could be, and the chil - dren say he could
Snow Man had to hur - ry on his way, but he waved good - bye say - in',

laugh and play just the same as you and me.
"Don't you cry, I'll be back a - gain some day."

Thump - et - y thump thump, thump - et - y thump thump, look at Frost - y go.

Thump - et - y thump thump, thump - et - y thump thump, o - ver the hills of snow.

Sleigh Ride

Music by Leroy Anderson
Words by Mitchell Parish

First note

Verse
Moderately, in 2

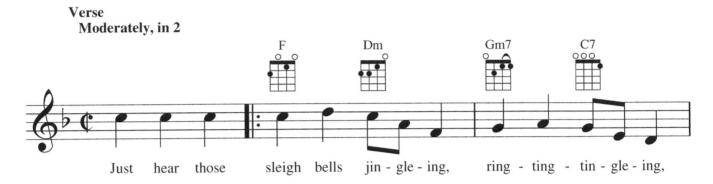

Just hear those sleigh bells jin-gle-ing, ring-ting-tin-gle-ing,

too. Come on, it's love-ly weath-er for a

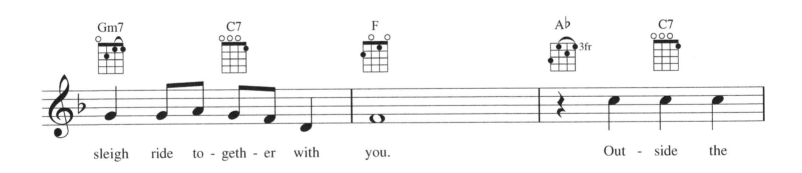

sleigh ride to-geth-er with you. Out-side the

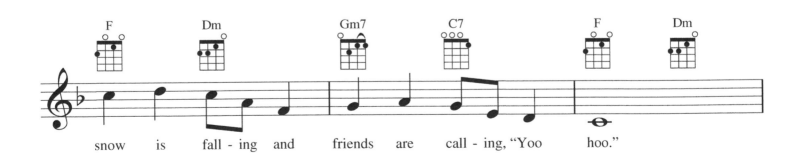

snow is fall-ing and friends are call-ing, "Yoo hoo."

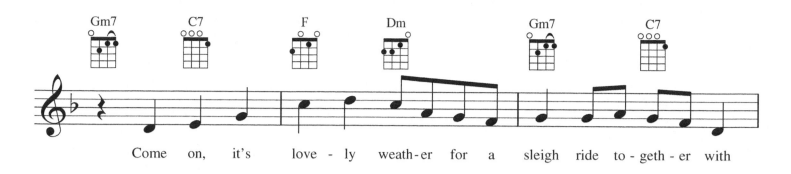

Come on, it's love - ly weath-er for a sleigh ride to - geth - er with

Bridge

you. _____ Gid - dy - yap, gid - dy - yap, gid - dy -

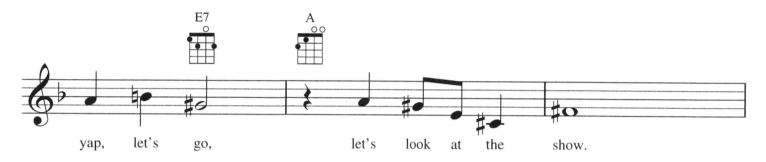

yap, let's go, let's look at the show.

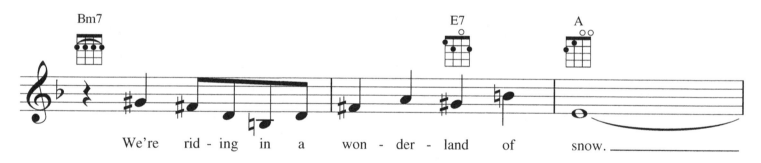

We're rid - ing in a won - der - land of snow. _____

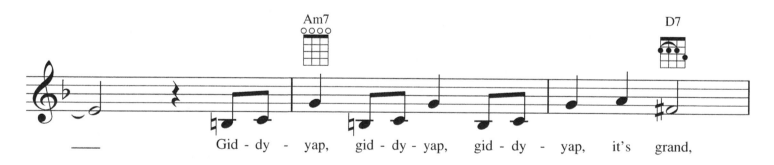

_____ Gid - dy - yap, gid - dy - yap, gid - dy - yap, it's grand,

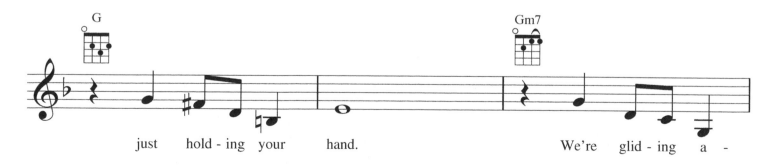

just hold - ing your hand. We're glid - ing a -

Outro-Verse

long with a song of a win-ter-y fair-y - land. Our cheeks are

nice and ros - y, and com - fy co-zy are we.

We're snug-gled up to-geth-er like two birds of a feath-er would

be. Let's take that road be - fore us and

sing a cho-rus or two. Come on, it's

love-ly weath-er for a sleigh ride to-geth-er with you. _____

Here We Come A-Caroling

Traditional
Arranged by Richard Friedman

bless   you   and   send ____ you   a   hap - py   New

Year,   and   God   send   you   a   hap - py   New   Year.

Interlude

Verse

3. We   have   got   a
(4.) bless   the   mas - ter

lit - tle   purse   of   stretch - ing   leath - er   skin.   We
of   this   house;   like - wise,   the   mis - tress,   too,   and

want   a   lit - tle   mon - ey   to   line   it   well   with -
all   the   lit - tle   chil - dren   that   'round   the   ta - ble

Deck the Halls

Traditional
Additional Lyrics by Robin Frederick

1. Deck the hall with boughs of hol - ly.
2. Friends and fam - 'ly come a - knock - ing.
3. Now the stock - ings come be - fore us.

Fa, la, la, la, la, la, la, la, la.
Fa, la, la, la, la, la, la, la, la. To
Fa, la, la, la, la, la, la, la, la.

'Tis the sea - son to be jol - ly;
help us hang our Christ - mas stock - ings.
Cel - e - brate them with a cho - rus.

Fa, la, la, la, Deck la, la, la, la.
Fa, la, la, la, la, la, la, la, la.
Fa, la, la, la, la, la, la, la, la.

G   C

Don   we   now   our   gay   ap - par - el;
High   on   wall,   on   gay   hearth   or   hang - er.
Fill   them   up   to   full   -   est   meas - ure.

Am   D7   G   C   G

Fa,   la,   la,   la,   la,   la,   la,   la,   la.   Troll   the   an - cient
Fa,   la,   la,   la,   la,   la,   la,   la,   la.   Red   and   green,   their
Fa,   la,   la,   la,   la,   la,   la,   la,   la.   Here   we'll   find   our

1., 2.

F   C   F   C   G

yule - tide   car - ol;   Fa,   la,   la,   la,   la,   la,   la,   la,
wool - en   splen - dor.   Fa,   la,   la,   la,   la,   la,   la,   la,
Christ - mas   treas - ure.

3.

C   G   F   G   F   C

la.   Fa,   la,   la,   la,   la,   la,
la.

G   C   F   C   G   C

rit.

la,   la,   la.   Fa,   la,   la,   la,   la,   la,   la,   la,   la.

Joy to the World

Words by Isaac Watts
Music by George Frideric Handel
Adapted by Lowell Mason

Jolly Old St. Nicholas

Traditional 19th Century American Carol

Additional Lyrics

2. When the clock is striking twelve, when I'm fast asleep,
   Down the chimney broad and black, with your pack you'll creep.
   All the stockings you will find hanging in a row.
   Mine will be the shortest one; you'll be sure to know.

3. Johnny wants a pair of skates, Susie wants a sled.
   Nellie wants a picture book: yellow, blue and red.
   Now I think I'll leave to you what to give the rest.
   Choose for me, dear Santa Claus; you will know the best.

Silent Night

Words by Joseph Mohr
Translated by John F. Young
Music by Franz X. Gruber

Away in a Manger

Words by John T. McFarland (V. 3)
Music by James R. Murray

First note

Verse
Sweetly

1. A - way in a man - ger, no crib for a bed, the
2. The cat - tle are low - ing, the Ba - by a - wakes, but
3. Be near me, Lord Je - sus, I ask Thee to stay close

lit - tle Lord Je - sus laid down His sweet head. The
lit - tle Lord Je - sus no cry - ing He makes. I
by me for - ev - er and love me, I pray. Bless

stars in the sky ___ looked down where He lay. The
love Thee, Lord Je - sus, look down from the sky and
all the dear chil - dren in Thy ten - der care and

lit - tle Lord Je - sus, a - sleep on the hay.
stay by my cra - dle 'til morn - ing is nigh.
fit us for heav - en to live with Thee there.

Christmas Together /
O Christmas Tree

Words and Music by Philip Baron

O CHRISTMAS TREE
Traditional
Additional Lyrics by Robin Frederick

Verse
Slower

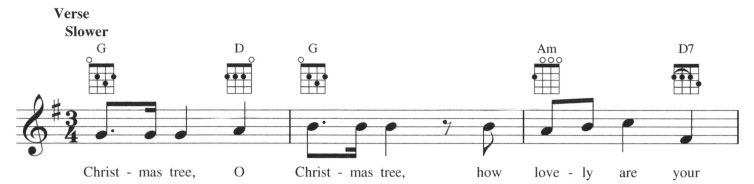

Christ - mas tree, O Christ - mas tree, how love - ly are your

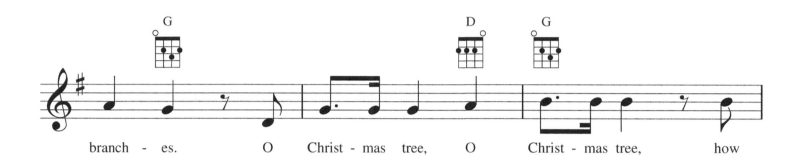

branch - es. O Christ - mas tree, O Christ - mas tree, how

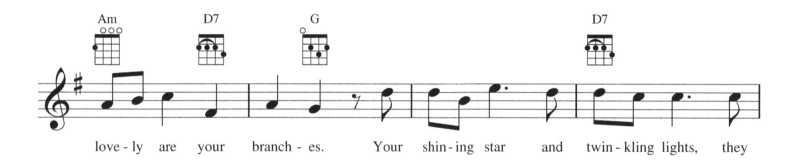

love - ly are your branch - es. Your shin - ing star and twin - kling lights, they

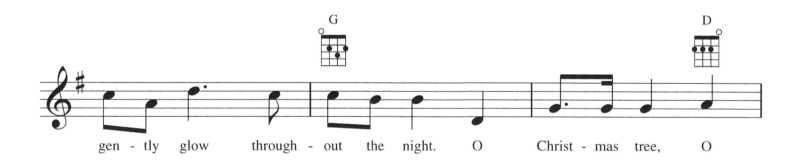

gen - tly glow through - out the night. O Christ - mas tree, O

Christ - mas tree, how love - ly are your branch - es.

Santa Claus Is Comin' to Town

Words by Haven Gillespie
Music by J. Fred Coots

Bridge

He sees you when you're sleep - ing, he knows when you're a -

wake, he knows if you've been bad or good, so be

Outro-Verse

good for good - ness sake. Oh! You bet - ter watch out, you

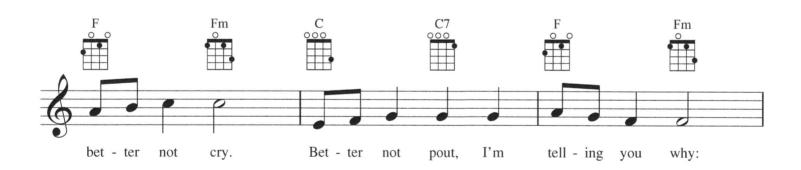

bet - ter not cry. Bet - ter not pout, I'm tell - ing you why:

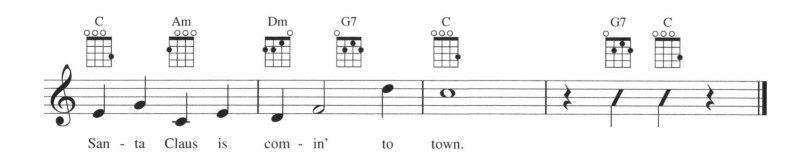

San - ta Claus is com - in' to town.

From All of Us to All of You

Lyrics by Gil George
Music by Paul J. Smith

First note

Verse
Bouncy 2-beat

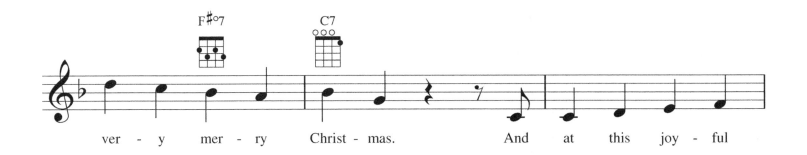

From all of us to all of you, a

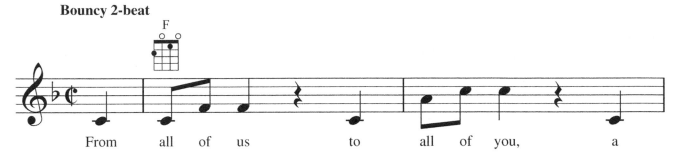

ver - y mer - ry Christ - mas. And at this joy - ful

time of year, we want you to be with us. So

gath - er 'round our love - ly tree, where all the lights are

shin - ing.   We'll   be   as   hap - py   as   can   be,   while

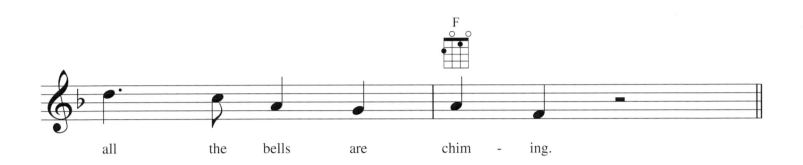

all   the   bells   are   chim   -   ing.

Chorus

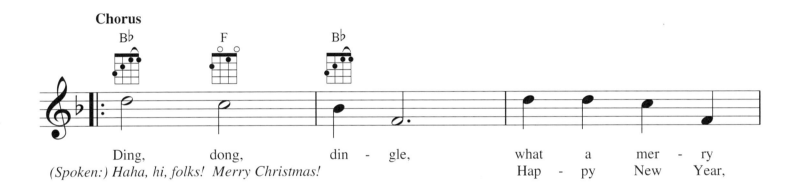

Ding,   dong,   din - gle,   what   a   mer - ry
(Spoken:) Haha, hi, folks! Merry Christmas!   Hap - py   New   Year,

sound.   Ding,   dong,   din - gle,   Kris
too.   *Haha, Merry, Merry Christmas!*   From

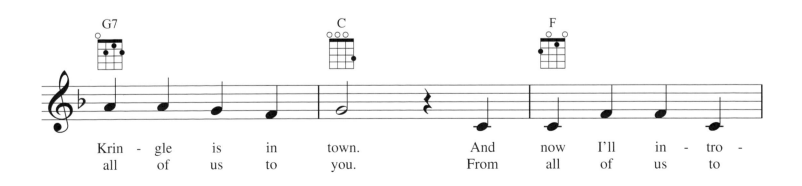

Krin - gle   is   in   town.   And   now   I'll   in - tro -
all   of   us   to   you.   From   all   of   us   to

duce   you   to   the   gang   that's   here   to   meet   you.   The
all   of   you,   can't   wait   un - til   you're   with   us.   We'll

1.

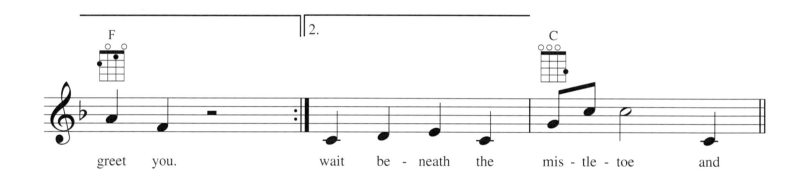

hap - py   house   of   Mick - ey   Mouse   is   wait - ing   here   to

2.

greet   you.   wait   be - neath   the   mis - tle - toe   and

Outro

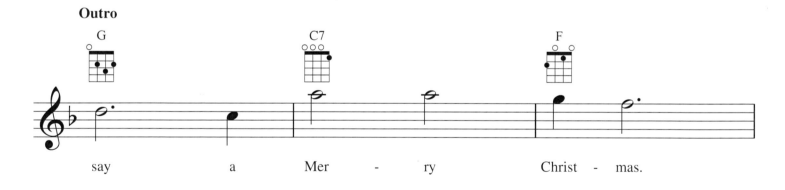

say   a   Mer - ry   Christ - mas.

We Wish You a Merry Christmas

Traditional
Arranged by Richard Friedman